Dierre and Patricia Glenn

UP-CLOSE & PERSONAL
From Living Single to a Healthy Marriage

Library of Congress Cataloging-in-Publication Data

Dierre Glenn and Patricia Glenn, Authors
Up Close and Personal

Anthony KaDarrell Thigpen, Publisher

ISBN-13: 978-0-977769773
1. Christians - Religious Life, Self-Help, Marriage
Printed in the United States of America

Published by
Literacy in Motion

TABLE OF CONTENT

TABLE OF CONTENT Continued

Session 1
THE DATING GAME

WHERE IT ALL BEGINS

Up Close and Personal reveals the intimate details of a husband and wife pastoral team. Together, we've joined forces and combat the enemy's strategy against healthy marriages. Our openness, honesty and transparency concerning our own experiences have helped countless marriages triumph. Now, we're sharing 28-years of details about our marriage with readers and listeners around the globe. We know that God has given us a mantle to help build healthy marriages. The Bible is a sure guide for building such productive relationships. Our book is intended to make God's perspective practical and applicable for modern day marriages. As you read this book you will hear both of our voices blended together revealing our experiences Up Close and Personal. This chapter is where it all begins – the dating game.

In order to help singles avoid not-so-obvious tricks and traps, we allowed members of our congregation to conduct "question and comment" sessions during our "Up Close and Personal Seminars." Included in this chapter of the book are the results of those life-changing sessions.

WHAT IS THE PURPOSE OF SHACKING?

Shacking is when couples try to sample the cow rather than buying it. It is when an unwed couple takes up residence together, prior to making a life-long commitment. According to the National Center for Health Statistics, Recent studies reflect that 40-percent of people who live together at the start of a relationship never actually wed. Perhaps that's something single men and women should consider before making such decisions. Ultimately, we need to be real with ourselves. Ask yourself, "Why live like a married couple, if I don't want to be married?"

SHOULD WOMEN SEEK AFTER MEN?

A woman should never seek a good man. Regardless of how tempting it may be. The problem with doing so is that it conflicts with God's agenda. The scripture says, "When a man finds a wife, he finds a good thing and obtains favor of the Lord." Many women disregarded God's agenda because they have their own. There are always consequences when we do things our way instead of God's way. Some women are naturally more aggressive in nature than some men, so they will approach, and even ask men to marry them. Women with aggressive personality types should be careful to allow men to "find" them.

In other words, regardless of who does the initiating, make sure you allow that man to "discover" or find the value of your virtue as a woman. Wherever men are, women will come, and the opposite applies, but women should allow men to discover their true identity.

HOW TO GO FROM LIVING SINGLE TO MARRIAGE WITHOUT DATING

It's not that Christians shouldn't date. We don't merely date like the secular people of the world. During the "old school" days, couples didn't date without chaperones. It's unfortunate that people don't think they need chaperones anymore, and that's exactly why so many people are falling into temptation now. As strange as it sounds, most modern-day believers don't think they need God involved during the dating phase of their relationships. this misconception couldn't be further from the truth. There is nothing wrong with casually dating, or getting to know a person, but the wisdom of God must be applied. Again, there is nothing wrong with dating. How else would you get to know a person? However, there is something wrong with singles dating multiple people at the same time, especially in the same congregations. This has been proven to lead to problems time and time again. Plainly stated, this is how a lot of unwanted chaos starts. All it takes is one date with the wrong person to create a total disaster out of your reputation.

WHEN DATING IN THE SAME MINISTRY, WHAT IS THE PROTOCOL?

Churchgoers should seek counseling from their own leaders concerning dating protocol. Never assume a ministry is too large or too small to have such discrepancies. All ministries should have dating protocols in place in order to prevent ministries from transforming into social gathering places. The church is not a club where anything goes, or at least it should not be anyway.

Worship services are for people to get spiritually fed, not to socially mingle. We have to keep our priorities straight. Protocols are not intended to control people or to manipulate singles into getting married sooner. Protocols are for those small areas that the Bible says little or nothing about. Considering the impact of ever-changing cultures on the religious community, pastors must use wisdom to help parishioners avoid tricks and traps. Without such protocols, singles will date in churches no different from how they date in secular society. As a result, without such wisdom, churches would be social melting pots. We'd produce unwed pregnant moms, absent fathers, and sexually transmitted diseases without godly protocol. However, we have to be careful not to allow changes in secular society to reflect upon the influences in the church.

The people who pose the problems with protocols are those who have been in the church the longest. Longevity can cause some people serious problems. Longevity causes people to think they can do things their own way. For example, a chaperone shouldn't be considered a third-wheel. In fact, there should be a third party when dating, the Lord Jesus. Dating is for two people only, plus the Lord. There are some pastors, and other people, who have wives, girlfriends, and baby mothers all in the same congregation. Do not be deceived because someone appears spiritual. Salvation does not mean you have everything "all together." People fall out of grace everyday, because of our flesh, no one is exempt – not even leaders. We are not strong enough to handle certain situations, and neither are you. "Can a man take fire in his bosom and his clothes not be burned?" Even the people with longevity get burned, despite the fact that they don't think they can.

If the situation presents itself at the wrong time - and the enemy packages temptation perfectly - you will fall. Christians are not exempt from falling – we have not   arrived. Some people can't be taught this principle; therefore, they always fail to listen to the wisdom of protocol. Ministry is about doing things God's way, and not sneaking to do them your own way. When you are spiritually mature, which people who have longevity should be, you will then seek godly counsel from your spiritual leaders. There is nothing wrong with dating. How you date, and whether or not God is in the equation, are the questions one needs to ask.

HOW TO DEAL WITH THE OTHER MOTHER

You always have to have a mutual respect when dealing with other people. When you neglect your children, or re-fuse to pay child support, you cannot be in right standings with God. Sometimes in life, we all do foolish things, es-pecially during our younger years. Are you willing to pay the price?

Regardless of age, we have to pay for our actions. After 23-years of paying child support, the total expense was more than $270,000. The courts realized that we'd paid $10,000 more than the allotted amount. We received an unexpected refund. I purchased a lot and built my wife a new house from the ground up. My wife respectfully dealt with the mother of my other children, during difficult moments, and during the great times. She also encouraged me to take care of my financial responsibility of paying child support. In the end, making wise choices paid off.

Session 2
TRANSPARENCY

IN THE BEGINNING

Our goal with this book is to be open, honest, and transparent with couples, both dating and married. So, you should know that we dated before we got married. In fact, we were high school sweethearts who met at the church that we both attended. After high school we spent about 6-months apart. Pastor Pat lived in Europe for about 6-months, before coming home to Gary, Indiana. Upon returning from Europe, we thought we were in love, so we decided to live together. Neither of us saw anything wrong with living together, at the time. We felt as though we were grown, he was my man, and I was his woman, and whatever we did was between him and me – so we thought. Never leave God out of your equation.

WHEN GOD CAME TO VISIT OUR SHACK

As the story goes, we were living together – shacking – that's what most church folks call it. After a couple of years, I stumbled across I Corinthians chapter 7, concerning every man having one wife and every woman having one husband. The Spirit of God started making me uncomfortable with our living situation. Like most people, I didn't respond to God initially. It wasn't until one night, when the Spirit dealt with me so strongly, that I started crying and weeping uncontrollably. With no uncertainty, God was visiting me. Eventually, I went to visit a local church. God was setting me up, so much that the speaker seemed to be talking directly to me.

This particular church service was the turning point of my lifestyle. It wasn't one of those churches where I could remain comfortable in my sin. That day, I sincerely dedicated my heart to God during service. Upon leaving, I was afraid to go home to Dierre – back then, he lived life as a gangster, not a pastor. I had no idea how to deal with him. I was fearful. But I knew when I got home I needed to say, "You have to go!" My drive home was filled with anxiety. I was scared, but I prepared myself to have the conversation that would change our lives forever. For the first time, I realized God is with me, and I have to stand for Him.

The moment I walked through the door he said, "Where have you been?" He was staring at me aggressively! Years later, I learned that he knew something was different about me.

I replied, "I went to church."

"I know that" he yelled out! "What church?"

I wasn't even sure of the name of the church. "But guess what" I said! "I got saved today!" He replied, "You got

17

what?"

"I gave my life to the Lord," I said with a sense of excitement. "And guess what?"

He asked, "What?"

Calmly I said to him, "What we're doing is wrong."

He asked again, "What?"

I remained calm and repeated myself, "What we are doing is wrong, and you have to go. We are not living right."

He slammed his fist on the table, and then aggressively yelled, "How you going to go to church, and in 2-hours somebody going to just change your mind about somebody that you been saying you love for years? And now you telling me, 'I got to go?'"

I said, "Yea."

"Well guess what? I ain't going no where," he screamed while throwing things in his rage.

I replied, "I really mean it. I got saved, and I'm living my life for God."

Dierre was extremely upset. He continued slamming things, but finally he agreed to leave. He asserted that there must be a man of interest at the church – as if some other man had gotten my attention. He accused me of losing my mind. We threw his clothes in garbage bags, and he called a friend to help him move all his belongings.

Still yelling, Dierre screamed, "I'm taking everything in here that's mine."

"You can have it all," I said.

After loading the truck with his belongings, he came in to say goodbye.

I calmly replied, "Take care."

Suddenly, out of no where, this strong, hard, and masculine man started weeping and crying so broken-heartedly. He broke down, and so did I.

I told him I was sorry for hurting him, but I didn't want to live in sin anymore. He kissed my cheek and left.

STAND FOR SOMETHING OR FALL FOR ANYTHING

What I admire most about Pastor Pat is that she took a stand. Most women and men aren't standing for God anymore. Don't compromise God's plan for your life. Years later, I thanked her for not compromising. Always remember, "thank you" may not be the first response you might get. It certainly wasn't my first reaction. Three months past, and I went to shack with another women, even though my heart was with Pat. The situation with this woman was worse. Here's why. I felt like she was dogging me. As I recall, one night I was sitting up waiting on her to come home, and she was gone for 2-days. Remember, you reap what you sow. And then another night, I was sitting up reminiscing about Pat. This was what I call a "double hurt."

I was so wounded that I went out and bought me a fifth of "something," and fired up a couple of joints. Have you ever been so hurt that you couldn't even get high? I was definitely drunk, but I didn't feel any better. I could barely walk, but I said to myself, "I'm going down to that church and I'm going to find this man." I was convinced Pat left me for some guy at the church. Completely drunk, I walked into the church, and sat on the back row of a Bible study. I was so drunk that I just sat there real "cool like" — just ignorant. Pat walked right by me. I barely even recognized her. Her hair was fixed-up, she had on make-up, and was even wearing a dress. I'd never seen her like that. She even had a glow. God had transformed her. After taking a double-look, I just broke down crying. ...And to think, she just walked right pass me. She was helping some woman and then bent over – my mouth dropped. I didn't even have time to get jealous about the suspected man; I just knew I wanted whatever she had spiritually. Afterward, the preacher started preaching emphatically about being born again. As a result, he blew any sense of high I did have.

"You know you been hurt," he yelled!

"You know you need Jesus to come into life your life."

It was as if he was singing, talking, and yelling all at the same time, "He's the only one that can heal you from your hurts." Some words he stretched out and made them extra long, "Is there 'ANYONE HERE' tonight that need the Lord to come into your 'LIFE.'"

And after all that hard and long preaching, and placing emphasis on every syllable, the brothers of the church embraced Dierre, but he still didn't get saved. He slipped out after telling me how good I looked. He also said he really liked what the preacher was saying. It wasn't long after that I went back and got saved. Well, I gave my life to the Lord, but I wasn't filled with the Spirit of God. I recall several months before God brought us back together. I was laid off from US Steel, and I really didn't even have anywhere to lay my head, but we still didn't compromise. About 3-months later, we decided to get married. Now that we took a stand for Christ, our entire dating experience became renewed. We were so serious about marriage, and pleasing God, that we got married immediately following a mid-week Bible Study. We've been married every since, and during these 28-years we've never been separated.

BLENDED FAMILIES ARE BEAUTIFUL TOO

By the time we married, I had one daughter outside of marriage with Dierre; he had two other daughters and one son out of wedlock. After marriage, we had two more children together – a daughter and our youngest son. Most importantly, God blessed us to raise and support all 6-children as a beautifully blended family. Being a single mother and dealing with a husband who has other children equipped me to talk to other women who share similar stories. God allowed me to go full circle – from single parenting and shacking to stepchildren, and marriage. Now, when I share the word of God with others, many people relate and realize that if God did it for us, then He can do it for them. Men, don't allow your children, not even those from previous relationships, to come between you and your wife. Women, don't allow your children, not even those from previous relationships, to come between you and your husband.

DON'T ALLOW THE DEVIL TO TAKE ADVANTAGE OF YOUR SINGLENESS

As a man, I want women to know they should never sale themselves or lower the standard of being a virtuous woman. A virtuous woman, among other things, is one that doesn't compromise. She holds her body to the highest esteem. She has to be married to the Lord. Single women should know that the devil knows your weakness – baldhead, tall, and good-looking. Once an ungodly or lustful man sees that twinkle in your eyes, he knows that you're the right prey. So, submit to God, and resist the devil, and you won't have to blend a family, you'll be able to just make one. Once you fall you lose some spiritual ground. Wait on the Lord. If you want a husband, the best person to tell is God. Meanwhile, watch out for the cologne, beware of the old flames, and don't allow the kitchen to get too hot. Remember, the title of this book is Up Close and Personal.

DIVORCED AND SINGLE AGAIN

If you've been divorced, allow your hurt to turn you into a better person. There are two types of abuse, mental and physical. Mental abuse at times is worse than physical abuse. Sometimes, there is no escape except divorce, specifically when your life is at jeopardy. If God set you free from something that was holding you hostage and captive, you should be shouting about your freedom. Divorces that are caused by addictions, whether it is through alcoholism, drugs, or sexual addictions, can be the worse. In these cases, you can still be in love with someone, but their actions will force you to leave them. Some people will literally drive you to divorce. Some relationships are so bad that there is no future to them – a complete waste of time – and then before you know it, you're old and still single. Sometimes God will remove you from a relationship, because He has a greater purpose for your life. Regardless of why you are single now, God wants you to know that you cannot get to the next level with weights. If you plan to marry someone, it should be through sickness or health, better or for worse, and for richer or for poorer. People are not going to look or move the same in 30-years. Make decisions based on the will of God, not carnal-lustful desires. Bad decisions lead to divorce. If a person is not adding or multiplying in your life, then they are subtracting and dividing. No one needs negativity and stress in life. And singles must remember not to marry out of loneliness. Unfortunately, men and women both fall prey to this trap. Men get hurt, too. In fact, it is sometimes easier for a woman to get back up, than it is for a man to recover from a divorce. I've counseled men that take a lifetime to overcome the tragedy of divorce. This is why the most important quality to look for in a person is to make sure that they love God. If he/she doesn't love God, then he/she won't love you. And if you can get them in the bed to compromise their relationship with God, then he/she will compromise their relationship with you. Anybody that pulls you away from God is not sent from God. If he/she is not faithful to God, then that person is not going to be faithful to you.

WISDOM FOR SINGLE MEN

Men need to look for women that see their better qualities. A moment of pleasure is not enough to make a decision about a wife. In fact, that moment of pleasure shouldn't even happen prior to marriage. Beware of distractions. Unfortunately, too many women are looking for a "sugar daddy" and security. Most women know how to catch men in a snare of lust. Men need to be careful about settling based on physical appearance or sexual desire. Beware of the flesh. Men and women alike, make poor temporary decisions that can cause permanent lifetime consequences.

Transparency /Session 2

Session 3
Get Your Priorities In Order

SPICE IT UP

It's important for married men to understand that their wives are their first priority after God – not the church, not your vision, and not your ministry. A lot of our pastor friends forget their priorities. They spend more time at the church and doing ministry work than they do with their wives. We've met women, even pastor's wives, who hated the church, because they blamed the church for taking their husbands away. It's easy for men in ministry to forget their first title and first ministry is being a husband. When I'm at home I don't walk around in a suit and tie, I walk around in my sexy underwear. I say this jokingly, but I'm trying to give other men a heads-up. Likewise, women of God need to also realize that your spouse should know you better than anyone. Show me who you are at home, and then we can discover the "real" you. Women, remember, come out of the footed pajamas. He doesn't want to encounter Fort Knox.

MARITAL RESPONSIBILITIES

When your man of God is unhappy, then the woman of God needs to figure out why. After all, God created you to help him. In some cases, this unhappiness is because of something the woman is lacking. Men have needs. God says it is not good for men to be alone. God pulled the woman out of the man's rib or side. It has always been God's intent that the man and woman walk side-by-side in effort to compliment one another. Also, it is a man's responsibility to embrace and protect his wife. When women feel like their husbands aren't doing their job, they began to act in ways that is not the "Proverbs 14:1" type of woman. Although we have to encourage our husbands regardless of how we feel. Pastor Dierre has been an awesome provider and protector, because his life lines up with the Word of God. He once said, "I'm going to make sure my children have what they need, even if I have to die trying." One spouse cannot tear the house down while the other is trying to build it. Wives must realize that God created them to support their husbands. This is why I serve my husband as unto the Lord. When was the last time you encouraged your husband by telling him he did a good job? When was the last time you've told your husband that you really appreciate everything he does? In fact, when was the last time you told him, "You look really good today?" A wise woman must be the cheerleader of her home. We must say things like, "You are the king of this castle, how was your day, or can I fix something for you to eat?" You must keep the fire burning. Men, remember women are moved by their heart. As a result, words carry weight. The reason a greater percentage of marriages are attacked amongst believers, is because the devil desires to destroy God's plan for family.

THE GIFT OF MARRIAGE

"Up Close and Personal" seminars are an entity of "We Are One" (WAO Enterprises). One of the gifts that God has imparted in us is the gift of Marriage. Did you know that marriage is a gift? It is. And we must embrace it as such. "Up Close and Personal," the book, is a series of seminars designed to strengthen singles, build healthy marriages and allow readers an opportunity to dialog about intimate issues in a godly setting. And so, we agreed, "Rather than to do it in private one-on-one settings all the time, we decided to get a group of people together and basically open our lives and share our personal experiences to the glory of God."

EVERY TESTIMONY BEGINS WITH A TEST

We have not been in God all of our lives; meaning we have not always had a relationship with Him. We were together before we encountered Christ, and enjoy sharing with the world how our relationship is nothing like it was before Christ. When Christ comes into your life he will change how you think and what you do, if you allow him to. We have been married for 28 years. Now if you ask, "Have your lives been 'honkey-dorey,' apple pie, smooth as ice cream, or even peaches?" I would have to say no it hasn't. However, we can tell you since Christ has been in our lives, God has given us the tools needed to work hard at strengthening our marriage. Did you know that marriage requires hard work? We have allowed God to give us guidance and to personally show us how to have a healthy marriage. Our marriage has been perfected in Christ. You should also remember that before we gave our lives to Christ, we lived together - we shacked – as most people refer to cohabitating couples that are not married. As a result, I asked God why did He handpick us for this particular ministry. He said, "I'm going to let you both experience something." It reminds me of when Jesus endured earthly experiences so that He could relate to us – and so that we could relate to Him. Although it is important to remember that Jesus did no sin, he merely took on the sins of the world. Nevertheless, our testimony is no secret – we shacked, as we've stated before. We also have children outside of marriage. Before we married, together we had one daughter, and we have three other children that Pastor Dierre fathered outside our relationship. We refer to all of them as "our children," because his children are my children. One of the greatest things you can have in life is family - and a family unit is

31

not going to be any stronger than the husband and wife of each household. Whatever comes out of them is what's going to pour and trickle down to their offspring. If your marriage is not currently functioning well, it's not too late – it's never too late. At any stage of your situation, you can allow God to come in and do something spectacular in your marriage. Prayer is the starting point that will allow the entire family to live in order based on the things of God.

LIVING SINGLE

One of the key components of getting to this point is open dialogue about very explicit things as it relates to being single. Most pastors do not to talk about the personal pitfalls of their own testimony, especially as it relates to the choices they made when they were single. In most cases, you really don't know about their lives prior to becoming pastors. However, it is important to remember this critical principle; Devastating things always happen to individuals that have a special gift or calling on their life before they reach their potential destiny. The devil tries to abort Gods will, plan, and purpose for your life. This especially happens to people who are single, because the enemy wants you to repeatedly make the kind of mistakes that will keep you down emotionally and spiritually. We are here to set the record straight – the devil can't knock you down any lower than your knees. On your knees, positioned for prayer, is exactly where God wants you. We have a strong sense of admiration and certain degree of respect for singles, or unwed believers living for God. Most people that remain single after they have met God have been previously hurt and/or wounded. Even though God has taught them how to forgive, they still don't quite feel as if they could ever love again. The devil is liar. (Repeat those words with us). "The devil is a liar." God is the only author and finisher of our faith. You can love again and you can trust again. Happiness starts from within. When you fall to your knees and present yourself before the throne of God, He will give you the desire of your heart. Don't ever stop believing in love. Don't settle for just anything, because most of us have done that. It doesn't make good sense to get in God and continue getting what you got when you were in the world. Be careful of the imitators and perpetrators that aim to duplicate Christianity. People are quick to say they are Christians, but your lifestyle speaks volumes. A lot of men used to come to church just to get women, and these days women also come to get men. Be careful, because once you've said "I do" these imitators will reveal their identity overnight – it will seem as though they've transformed into a monster. You'll find yourself in a position whereas you will get what you want, but you will lose what you had. This concept has everything to do with the teachings of the Apostle Paul in the book of Corinthians – be not unequally yoked. Do you know when somebody isn't equally yoked with you?

GUARD YOUR HEART

Never race back to bad relationships. Some people seem to be drawn to negativity and abuse. Learn how to see yourself the way God sees you. God never intends for you to be on rewind. Personally, we choose to live our life together in fast forward. Rewind means nothing is changing but the outward appearance. Abuse comes in all faces, forms, and facets. The worse form of abuse is mental abuse. There's nothing like peace, and mental abuse is a direct assault on God's promise of peace. The next abuse is verbal. If a man or a woman won't love God, then guess what? They can't love you either. The Bible describes this artificial love as sounding of brass and tingling cymbals – lots of noise. We hope and pray for singles to understand and take possession of patience. Patiently take your desires, goals, and ambitions before God and leave them. Your mate will come when you least expect it. It's going to be somebody that God will connect you with. She may not have the 24-inch waistline you're looking for, or vice versa. Without question, your spouse is going to be somebody that God will place in your life that will enhance you spiritually. Why would God connect you with someone that will ruin your gift, tear you down mentally, verbally, physically, naturally, and practically? That isn't the will or plan of God. God doesn't want you to be married to a demon. You've interacted with enough demons while you were living a secular lifestyle. Once you've been set free, continue to live free from the schemes and tricks of the enemy. If the person of interest does not demonstrate their daily love for God, you're wasting your time. And don't think you can change them. You can't change anybody, only God can, and even then they must be willing.

MARRYING FOR THE WRONG MOTIVES

Women of God, the worse thing you can do is marry for security, the only security you should have is in Jesus. Perhaps you're wondering why? When the smoke clears and the dust settles, what you thought was security suddenly reveals itself as the thing you actually need protection from. Relationships based on security never stand the test of time. However, if you marry somebody because of the love of God, which reveals itself from the inside, then God will be the focal point of your relationship. It is far better to marry somebody who loves God than someone with all the money in the world, so to speak. Don't make your decisions or set your standards based on money. If that is the case, you are losing before you even get started. You can go a whole lot further in your marriage if you approach situations with the right perspectives – get your priorities straight while you're still single. Oftentimes, the devil uses this trick to get you distracted from the things of God, and hooked up for all the wrong reasons, because all you see are dollar signs. You see the dollar signs before you get married, then what usually happens afterward, someone loses a job, or doesn't have the money you thought. As a result, your marriage is built upon an optical illusion. The second pitfall singles spring into is good looks. Perhaps they look good on your arm, but you can't marry for looks and actually expect the relationship to last. Guess what? Everybody will change. We all age, some more gracefully than others. A woman's figure is likely to change, and six packs often turn into inner tubes. So, don't marry because of good looks, waistlines, good hair, muscles or anything physical. These are the wrong reasons to get married. Statistics have proven that if you marry for money and/or security the marriage doesn't usually last more than three years. Once all the money is spent – the artificial love is gone. Men must especially be aware of this, if not, you are likely to get hurt as well.

GOD'S PLAN FOR FINDING A SPOUSE

Put God's promises to the test. Men of God, the word clearly states that when you find a wife, you find a good thing. Afterward, you will obtain favor from the Lord. Herein the standard is set for single women. Virtuous women do not chase after men. Such behavior is not scriptural, biblical or godly. There's a certain standard set when a person has the Holy Ghost, as to how to present himself or herself as a vessel of God. There's a certain mystique that a virtuous woman is supposed to possess - and it doesn't stop there. A virtuous woman has standards. When you know who you are in God, you don't have to lower your standard to attract anyone.

HOW RESPECT CAN SAVE A MARRIAGE

What does a husband need most from his wife? Husbands need respect, support, sex, honesty, encouragement, a listening ear, patience, prayer, communication, obedience to God, and most importantly love. However, according to most literature, respect is number one. When you respect your spouse everything else will fall in place. Respect means to honor, reverence, and be sensitive to ones needs. Having the respect that we've described, is the main ingredient for a healthy marriage. Understand that your respect enables him to be a man that knows he can come to his wife with anything, from painful problems and secret situations, to ever-changing circumstances. A virtuous woman is there to respect and let her husband know it's going to be all right. A husband should never feel that he is going through something alone. Neither should he feel he has to deal with life's challenges by depending on his buddies, mother, friends, and daddy to get some satisfaction. The greatest encourager a man wants to depend on is his wife. The only reason why he wouldn't confide in you is because he feels you are not going to respect his opinion. Just as much as sex, a man wants respect.

BEWARE OF THIRD PARTIES

Here's a little twist, third parties should never play a role in your marriage. Sometimes, when the respect level isn't there, somebody else is willing to lend an ear. This happens when a woman is so shut down that she doesn't respect her spouse, won't listen to him, and consistently nags him. All too often, a woman will ask God for a husband, and then not know what to do with him once she says "I do." During seasons when the wife is inappreciative, the devil sends Susie. She knows all your business, because she's listening to him, because he poured out his heart to her, and primarily because you wouldn't listen. Always remember, there is someone else who wants your spouse. Learn to listen to your mate.

CONTROL FREAKS

Men, don't shut down. And never assume you have all the answers. Some men think they have to be in control. This is called a "control freak." First, learn how to manage your own home, rather than trying to control others. Even worse, is a husband who attempt to control his wife. Such behavior is not acceptable, nor is it biblical. Women are often scared to say anything to insecure control freaks. As a result of 20-years of counseling, we've heard it all.

Session 4
Selfless Sacrifices

BOTH SPOUSES HAVE NEEDS IN MARRIAGE

A wife will often cry out to someone else if it isn't you, and it may not always be her girlfriends. Men of God, when God blesses you with a wife, don't make her liable for the mistakes other women made in your past relationships. We do not like marrying people that bring skeletons from their past relationships. When you're married, all walls need to come down. God's intent for husbands and wives is for them to be inseparable. We are supposed to be so close with our spouses that no one can tell us anything about them. Keep the enemy out of your marriage. Learn how to walk in admiration; loving each other without the walls. Don't marry someone you can't trust. Stop being insecure, you have no need to worry. Rest in the things of God. There should be no insecurity if somebody else compliments your spouse. Be secure in your relationship. Don't disrespect one another. Saying things in the heat of the moment requires wisdom. Some comments you will never be able to take back. People remember exactly what you've said, especially when your words hurt to the core. Don't let the sun go down upon your wrath. Don't find yourself sleeping in other bedrooms and on couches. Women stop protesting with no dinners, no lunches, and no sex. Remember, the "real man" is not the leader or the brother at church, much rather it's the husband, father and man at home. Respect is also about feeling valued, needed, and important. Feeling valued means that the husband has a sense of importance to his wife. A woman is supposed to make a man feel needed and valued. How should a woman make her husband feel valued? Most importantly, she really needs to make him feel like he's the king of the castle. The wife is the queen, and the queen does not overthrow the king. Encourage him, be submitted, be a blessing to him, making him feel loved, and be sensitive to his needs. Keep the word "no" out of your vocabulary and a "yes" in your heart.

INTIMACY IS A GIFT FOR MARRIAGE

It's important to keep the bedroom open. In other words, women, unless there's a logical reason, your husband should never have to ask for intimacy. You should be able to look into his eyes and discern. Don't be scared to serenade your mate. Allow your music of choice to serve as your Viagra. There are little things that signify that the heat of the moment is about to catch on fire. Men, don't rush the moment – take your time. Take your time and wait for the volcano to slowly erupt.

You have to keep the fire burning in your marriage. When the fire slowly diminishes the door opens for the enemy. Know how to throw more coals on the fire so that it will not go out. When there is no more fire, people often go outside their marriages for intimacy. Even couples of this world know how to keep their mates satisfied. Don't get "so saved" that you lose your mate. Some people are indeed heavenly bound, but no earthly good.

DEEP IN THE BEDROOM

Whether a woman can have children or not has nothing to do with the way you love her. You married her for her, not for children. What goes on in the bedroom chambers is between you, your spouse, and God. Some things married couples don't expose to anybody. If you like kinky, and your spouse is in agreement, then there's nothing wrong with it. God knows what you want, and He will send you exactly what you need.

GOD IS THE AUTHOR OF MARRIAGE

God established the institution of marriage. This sacred union has been in place since the foundation of the world. Don't allow the enemy to dictate, distract, and defeat you with his ideologies about marital relationships. God Himself has given us every available tool for marriage. The world should be looking at the marriages in the church. Instead, churchgoers have a higher divorce rate than secular minded people. As a result, nonbelievers stick with their approach on shacking, in part, because of the poor examples set by believers. Don't forget how to love each other. The world should look at marriages in the church and desire to have what we have. People of God, we must learn how to value our marriages. For us, it is a great experience to have singles seeking God and allowing Him to send them mates in the church. You shouldn't expect anyone to love you if they don't know how to love God first.

KEEP THIRD PARTIES OUT OF YOUR MARRIAGE

Many people have questions about the consequences of including third parties in their relationships. So, it is important for us to recap and remind you that some marriages never bounce back from third parties. Third parties are most often a result of wounds, hurt feelings, immaturity, and insecurities. The devil knows when there is a crack in your heart, and he tries to enter. Instead of going to third parties, seek godly counsel, godly professionals with discretion, as soon as you can, don't wait. The blame should not all be on the spouse with indiscretions, if the other spouse is being negligent in the relationship. Third parties dig deeper into wounds preventing them from ever healing. People will try to sabotage your relationship for various reasons, whether you're single or married. Women, never talk to other men more than you talk to your own husband. Men, never talk to other women more than you talk to your own wife.

Session 5
Marrying the Right Person

WHAT TO LOOK FOR IN A SOULMATE?

If it's of God, you're going to know when you've found your soul mate. First off, you should check their family history. Remember this advice when considering your options, "If it's in the root, then it's in the fruit." Knowing a person's background is important. As a single woman, you need to know that men play games. Don't get beat. Don't be desperate for any man. Stay at peace when God brings your soul mate. A soul mate is more than just a friend. She/He will respect you as a virtuous woman or a God-fearing man. Nobody will be able to sabotage your relationship when you do things God's way. You can't sabotage what God has put together. When you really know your soul mate, can't a devil in hell sabotage your relationship!

AVOID INSECURITIES

Don't allow longevity in your marriage to determine how you feel about your spouse. The love should grow greater as time passes. The relationship should get even better as you grow older together. By the first five years you should know what you can and can't say to one another. The first five years are often the bumpiest in most marriages. You have to learn one another. If you know it angers your spouse, then don't say it. Don't become an old fool – grow in wisdom. Stop fighting and use your energy in loving. Insecurities will take you out of your character, and make you lose your mind. Insecurity can kill your marriage.

OVERCOMING ABUSIVE RELATIONSHIPS

God is not going to allow anything to stand in his way from getting you to your destiny. When you're in an abusive relationship God has ways of getting you out. Sometimes kids will get jealous, your husband is the king of the castle, and your wife is the queen. We can't even let our kids divide what God has joined together. Wives have to get out the way, even when it comes to the kids, whether biological or stepchildren. Don't allow kids to see discord in your marriage. Sometimes we marry people of opposite spirits. However, don't take kindness for weakness when your spouse has more grace than you. When the household is in order, unnecessary drama is often avoidable. However, husbands may not step up to the plate when their wives are always at the plate. Every man doesn't like to argue. Every man is not a fighter. If God gave you someone exactly like yourself you would be divorced. Normally extraverts are usually attracted to introverts. The right chemistry between individuals makes for healthy marriages. Men shouldn't be weak and jelly back.

God is not weak, and Jesus wasn't either. Some men like strong women. Be grateful and thank God for what He gave you. Learn to appreciate your differences instead of fighting about them.

DON'T BE UNEQUALLY YOKED

When you're equally yoked, the connection starts off with both parties desiring relationship revolving around pleasing God. Also, when you're praying together, studying together, giving thanks and praise to God, it causes both individuals to be submitted to God. There are qualifications to submitting. For example, an unbelieving spouse is not going to understand whom they are submitting to. The major requirement is walking in oneness, not in disagreement. Love one another, date, and give compliments. You can't invest your time arguing with one another and then expect submission. For example, insecurities affect the way you submit, or can cause you to not submit at all. Continue doing the acts of kindness you did when you met one another. How you start your day is how you end it. A woman "feels" with her emotions. Don't degrade her all day and then expect her to submit. The Bible doesn't just say, husbands submit to your wives, it says wives submit to your husbands. The part that is left out is "submitting yourselves one to another in the fear of

God" (Ephesians 5:21). Ask yourself, "Have you spent time with your wife?" On the other hand, have you been watching basketball and playing video games? Women don't want boys, they want men. These are factors you must consider prior to marriage.

UNDERSTANDING SUBMISSION

There are a lot of hurting men and women. So, remember, your mate is bone of your bone and flesh of your flesh. Be in love with your mate. Don't marry people just for the way they look, because your looks will change as the years go on. Be in love with your spouse. Love your wife as Christ loves the church. Men should find the wife, not the other way around. Marriage involves a relationship of mutual submission. That means submitting yourselves one to another as you both submit yourselves to God. It becomes unbalanced if only one practices this belief. Submit to one another in the fear of the Lord - Learn how to do so - it's not always easy. A marriage is a covenant relationship between two people. You're joined together by God, not by the preacher, so fear God. "In obedience to your command, we are going to dwell together in the fear of God," this should be our motto as married couples.

BIBLICAL PRINCIPLES FOR THE ENTIRE HOUSE-HOLD

Don't be afraid of one another. Walk together, build each other up, and encourage one another. There will be disagreements, but because you are joined together and submitting to God, you'll be able to come together and reason with one another. Not hearing from God, or each other, will create a big mess. Perfect marriages don't exist. When disagreements arise, someone has to submit to God. Learn how to walk together. Humble yourself. If you're married, submit to your own husband, not someone else. When people submit to their pastors, but not their spouses, it is out of order. And submission doesn't require conditions. Whether or not they have a job has nothing to do with the importance of remaining submitted. The husband is the head of the wife, according to scripture. What does the head do? The head determines the direction for everything else. He protects, shields, comforts, and provides. Husbands are essential. In today's society, a lot of women are running the household. God never intended for the woman to be the head of the household – that is also out of order. Children certainly should not run the house, or come in the middle of your marriage. These are biblical principles everyone should know.

GOD'S MANDATE ON MEN IN MARRIAGE

The head has to carry a lot of weight that women are not created to carry. Women are helpers. If women act as the head that means husbands have surrendered their role. "Mr. Mom" is not biblical. The Bible says men are to work by the sweat of their brow, and take care of their family. Women should learn to submit in everything not just in the bedroom. Don't label men based on your past relationships. Men are called "dogs" when they seek inti-mate fulfillment from other women outside the marriage. However, we have to look at the entire picture. Are you submitting to your mate in every way? The enemy tries to separate you at all costs, including using your own chil-dren. God ordained marriage. Marriage is good, although the world corrupts it. You can't base your marriage on anything other than the will and word of God.

Your marriage will be what the both of you make it. God joined husbands and wives to compliment each other. Marriage is a "give and take" communion. "What else can I do to make it better," or "How can I help?" Every hus-band should know his wife's limitations. That only comes with wisdom and paying attention to what your mate likes. A husband must make love to his wife's mind first. Every-thing is not wham bam thank you ma'am. Do not have the mindset that your mate is always ready. A woman's mind is not like a light switch — You can't turn it off and on so quickly.

IMPORTANT QUESTIONS SINGLES NEED TO ASK

Children: Do either of you have children, would you both desire to have children together, how will you discipline them, are you both willing to allow each other to discipline the step-children?

Money: How do you manage your money?

Sex: What type of history do you have?

In Laws: How much time and influence is coming from the in-laws?

Chores: How would you define roles, expectations, and responsibilities?

Time: How much quality time are you going to spend with me?

Addictions: Alcoholism, drug addict, sex addict, shopping and gambling?

Abuse: Have you ever been abused, or have you ever abused someone else?

Fidelity: Is this important to you?

Marriage: Is this forever, and do you believe in marriage?

PRINCIPLES TO LIVE BY

There has to be some ground rules set when blending children into one family. Don't let kids disrespect your mate. You are not married to your kids. Always seek Godly counsel. Forgive yourself for things done before Christ. Learn how to forgive yourself, so that you can move on to the next level. Sometimes the Lord allows you to go through things so that you're able to minister to others. Some of our greatest men and women of God are people that have gone through some of the worse challenges. Christ endured long-suffering and felt everything that we experience today.

We are nothing more than sinners who needed a Savior. The skillet can't call the kettle black. We all have experienced things in life. If you've never been married then God has to teach you how to be a husband or a wife. When a man finds a wife he finds a good thing. Not when a man finds a woman or a girlfriend. It takes the Spirit of God to be a good husband or wife. Strong marriages make great families, and children generally pattern their own lives after their parents. God explains how having a wife enables the husband to obtain a "good thing" and "favor." The Bible says it was not good for Adam to be alone, and that he needed a companion. Wives are supposed to be their husband's helpmeet. Every marriage should be built on the principles of God. Don't marry under false pretenses. Physical attractions are going to change as you go through life. To lead a family you have to know how to follow. Incline your ear to God so that he can show you. The favor of God will rest in your marriage when you line up with His Word. Release past relationships, even in your mind. Men and women of God need counseling before marriage so that they can learn the principles of God concerning godly marriage. Handle your business at home so that your mate isn't tempted to go outside the marriage. Although, it's important to remember, that a failing spouse is no excuse to commit adultery. Prayer is a necessity in any marriage. Embrace your mate - make your spouse feel her/his best. Build your mate up. Love your mate as yourself. Do not put your mate through anything you wouldn't want to go through.

TOUGH ADVICE THAT WORKS

Husbands love your wife as Christ loves the church. Christ loved the body of Christ so much that he died for us. Are you willing to die for your spouse? Learn how to communicate with your mate. Both men and women love to feel appreciated. No one likes to feel as though they're being taken for granted. Ask your spouse is there anything you need? Never make your mate feel like he/she is not needed. Don't always look at your mate's faults. A wise woman builds her house, and a foolish woman tears it down with her own hands. When you see your spouse getting frustrated and on the edge, check yourself first. The Bible says a foolish woman is the one that destroys her house. Before you get into marriage, you must seek Godly counsel. Divorced people need to forgive before they can move on to healthy relationships. Remember, only God can change a person and free them totally from their previous lifestyle and addictions. Let God change that person first. Don't keep making the same mistakes over and over. Everything that looks good and shines is not always the person you should be with. A person's heart, in the eyesight of God, is more meaningful than the outer appearance. You can marry a demon and not even know it, unless you put the principles of God's word into practice. Men and Women of God, don't compromise when it comes to making a decision about who you will spend the rest of your life with. You are of royal priesthood. So, don't settle for less than what God desires for you. There is somebody out there for you. God knows exactly what you need.

THE POWER OF A PRAYING WOMAN

Continue seeking God even when your spouse isn't interested. God does not want you in an abusive relationship, physically or mentally. Although, a sanctified woman sanctifies her husband. Therefore, being unequally yoked is not always grounds for separation. It is easy to give up on your marriage, but quitters never win. Pray for your spouse if they are not saved. Speak those things that are not as though they were. You must cover your mate's weakness. Sometimes people of God fail to do things God's way. Don't hinder the purpose and plan that God has for your life. Disconnect all relationships that aren't of God, but be sure to take into consideration the vows you made before God and witnesses. Keep Christ as the focus in your marriage. When a man sees that he can get between you and God, he loses a little respect for you. Virtuous women don't ever let a man take you away from the things of God. A virtuous woman is one who is not going to compromise her standard in Christ – continue praying. Hold your body upright, and let it be known that you are married to the Lord. As a single woman, the devil knows your weaknesses. He knows how to flatter you. Be careful, don't entertain it, resist the devil and submit to God. Always remember to approach everything with prayer.

MOVING FORWARD

The devil comes in all shapes, forms, and fashions; bald head and dreadlocks, clean-cut and rough-necks, tall and short, attractive and charming, and of course, great cologne. If you can get past this test, you'll have a testimony. Every person who falls don't always get back up the same way – this is why you must be careful. If you're single, be married to God. If you feel like your flesh is weak, pray, and then read the word of God. Tell God about your troubles and heartaches. When you tell Him, He will do something about it. Beware of past relationships that can remind you of the way you used to be. Don't marry just to keep your flesh satisfied. Marry because you know that's the one you're supposed to spend the rest of your life with. Sometimes hurt can make you better, when you allow God to heal your past. Always forgive. This will help you get over any past hurts and negative feelings. Time moves on, don't get stuck in your past. If a person doesn't add to your life, such as through encouragement, uplifting, multiplying, or seeing all the better qualities in you, then they are probably not the one. Singles, when you stumble and fall, don't let it keep you down. Get back up and move forward with the right perspective.

HOW TO WALK SIDE-BY-SIDE

A rib was taken from Adam's side, which first signifies that you walk side-by-side, even when you're apart. As a wife, it is your job to compliment your husband, just as it is his job to compliment you, both for different reasons. Husbands, we are supposed to cover our wives, protect, and to shield. A woman must be careful not to tear her husbands down while their trying to build the family up. A husband needs the support of his wife, and not only 59% of the time. Honor your husband, and submit to him as unto the Lord. When was the last time you gave your husband some encouragement? When was the last time you complimented him? That's how a wise woman builds her house. Always remember to remind him that he's the king of his castle. Men don't want to hear complaints and whining while having to deal with other issues in life. As a wife, have you ever asked him about his day before discussing the bills or disciplining the children? Don't let the fire go out, you must keep it going. Make your husband want to come home from work, not work overtime because he doesn't want to be at home with you. Keep the fire in your marriage women of God.

Biblical References

Page #	King James Reference
Page 9	PROVERBS 18:22
	Whoso findeth a wife findeth a good thing..
	PROVERBS 31:10
	Who can find a virtuous woman...
Page 12	PROVERBS 6:27
	Can a man take fire in his bosom...
	I CORINTHIANS 10:12
	Wherefore let him that thinketh he standeth...
Page 17-23	JAMES 4:7
	Submit yourselves therefore to God...
Page 27	GENESIS 2:18
	And the LORD God said, It is not good...
Page 28	GENESIS 2:22
	And the rib, which the LORD God...
Page 29-32	PROVERBS 14:1
	Every wise woman buildeth her house, but...
	PSALM 37:4
	Delight thyself also in the LORD...
Page 33	II CORINTHIANS 13:1
	Though I speak with the tongues of men...
Page 35	PROVERS 18:22
	Whoso findeth a wife findeth a good thing...
Page 40	EPHESIANS 4:26
	Be ye angry, and sin not: let not the s u n [

FOR MARRIAGE

and

SINGLE'S SEMINARS

WRITE TO:

ACKM-MC

1428 E. Michigan Blvd

Michigan City, IN 46360

OR CONTACT:

219-879-1962

219-878-7800

OR E-MAIL

pglenn1959@netzero.net

www.ingramcontent.com/pod-product-compliance
Lightning Source LLC
LaVergne TN
LVHW010025070426
835509LV00001B/13